Contents

Chapter One: Bitcoin 8
    Pre-history of Bitcoin 8
    Blockchain technology: the main driver behind the success of Bitcoin and cryptocurrencies 11
    Uses and theories of Bitcoin 12
    Bitcoin transactions 14

Chapter 2: Ripple 16
    Ripple at a glance 17
    The Ripple Protocol 18
    Difference between Bitcoin and other Altcoins 19

Chapter 3: Real world examples 22
    The safety of Bitcoin and Ripple 24
    Mining 27

Chapter 4: How to buy Bitcoin and Ripple 30

Chapter 5: How to store 35

Chapter 6: Before investing 38
    Investment mindset 38
    Paper profits vs. actual profits 42
    Special note on cryptocurrencies 45
    Long-term investing vs. day trading 45
    Investment/trading techniques 47
    Fundamental analysis 47
    Technical analysis 48

Averaging down 49

Pump and dump strategies 50

Governmental measures and policies on cryptocurrencies 50

Putting it altogether 51

Chapter 7: Who is the winner, Bitcoin or Ripple? 53

Thank you! 54

Other books in the series 55

Monero vs Bitcoin *The battle of the cryptocurrencies* 55

Ripple vs Bitcoin

The battle of the cryptocurrencies

By Johan von Amsterdam

Bitcoin vs. Ripple: An Introduction

You have probably heard of cryptocurrencies, Bitcoin, and Ripple. Every day you wonder what these things are and the impact they have on your life. Some have told you that you can become a millionaire if you really take it seriously. There are of course testimonies of Bitcoin millionaires all over the internet. Do these testimonies sound too good to be true?

As if that is not enough, there are theories that Bitcoin and Ripple are a new currency with the same functionality as your normal money. Can you really buy pizza or pay for your morning coffee with Bitcoin or Ripple? Moreover, Bitcoin and Ripple are just two of the coins. There are thousands more. Is there any place for all these coins? Is it worth it to know the differences between all the coins?

Cryptocurrencies rely on their underlying technology. What is the technology that gives these cryptocurrencies the attention that they have been getting? It does not matter whether you just heard of Bitcoin yesterday or last year, what you need is to the underlying technology and principles. Bitcoin or Ripple is not just ordinary money. It needs the right mental orientation to understand.

If the cryptocurrencies are a new form of money, then what are their differences with the current monetary system? It is difficult to trust transactions that are carried over the internet. The truth is that there are millions of scams on the internet. How can you be sure that Bitcoin, Ripple, and other similar currencies are not scams? How do you validate their legitimacy?

You are certainly interested in knowing how the coins are issued. Are there any central banks that determine how many coins must be released to the general public? Are cryptocurrencies regulated the same way that fiat money is? Is it safe? Is it secure? How anonymous is it?

Let's assume that you have given the cryptocurrencies the benefit of doubt and want to own them. Where do you get or buy them? This is the fundamental question that you should ask and get a straight and satisfactory answer. The question of money should never be left unanswered or half-answered.

There are of course promises made by the cryptocurrencies. These promises include very fast transactions. In the real world, we are used to cross-border payments that take up to 3 days. We now have Bitcoin that claims to process the same transaction in 10 minutes. If it is Ripple, they claim to process the same transaction in less than 3 minutes.

Ripple claims that cross-border payments cost people up to $1.6 trillion a year. The same currencies promise payment transactions that cost little to nothing. Is this feasible for them? What and how do they stand to gain from this?

The currencies are said to be decentralized and not owned or controlled by any central entity. This sounds great but is it safe and secure? Are they any better than banks? When banks started off, they gave us incentives for banking with them. When we were hooked with them and relied on them, they turned on us and charged us. Are cryptocurrencies not going to turn on us in the future?

The truth is that there is a lot to learn and know. This book will give you all the information you need to know about Bitcoin and Ripple. It will touch on their fundamental differences. It will also touch on their similarities such as decentralization, anonymity, near-zero transaction fees, speed, and security. This book answers all those questions and more.

A gift as a thank you!

The cryptocurrency world is a fast moving world.

If you want to stay up-to-date, please check out the author's website:

www.aboutcryptocurrencies.net.

Here you will find the latest cryptocurrencies news gathered from around the world and updated multiple times per day.

Sign-up for the 'Daily Crypto News' and receive the electronic version of the officially published book:

'Bitcoin: What is Bitcoin?'

for free as a thank you for buying this book.

- So go to www.aboutcryptocurrencies.net
- sign up
- get the 'Bitcoin: What is Bitcoin?' as a thank you.

And you know, only make educated decisions!

Yours sincerely,

Johan von Amsterdam

© Copyright 2018 - All rights reserved.

This document is geared towards providing exact and reliable information in regards to the topic and issue covered. The publication is sold with the idea that the publisher is not required to render accounting, officially permitted, or otherwise, qualified services. If advice is necessary, legal or professional, a practiced individual in the profession should be ordered.

- From a Declaration of Principles which was accepted and approved equally by a Committee of the American Bar Association and a Committee of Publishers and Associations.

In no way is it legal to reproduce, duplicate, or transmit any part of this document in either electronic means or in printed format. Recording of this publication is strictly prohibited and any storage of this document is not allowed unless with written permission from the publisher. All rights reserved.

The information provided herein is stated to be truthful and consistent, in that any liability, in terms of inattention or otherwise, by any usage or abuse of any policies, processes, or directions contained within is the solitary and utter responsibility of the recipient reader. Under no circumstances will any legal responsibility or blame be held against the publisher for any reparation, damages, or monetary loss due to the information herein, either directly or indirectly.

Respective authors own all copyrights not held by the publisher.

The information herein is offered for informational purposes solely, and is universal as so. The presentation of the information is without contract or any type of guarantee assurance.

The trademarks that are used are without any consent, and the publication of the trademark is without permission or backing by the trademark owner. All trademarks and brands within this book are for clarifying purposes only and are the owned by the owners themselves, not affiliated with this document.

Chapter One: Bitcoin

Bitcoin is very famous. I wouldn't expect any less from Bitcoin especially considering its paradigm shift in allowing secure transactions on its network. There are a few who really have no idea what Bitcoin is. There are, however, a few people who truly understand what Bitcoin is and what it can do. The point here is that there is a major difference between being aware of Bitcoin and knowing what it is. The aim of this chapter is to take elevate your awareness to knowledge. Knowledge is power. Our forefathers have held this mantra in high regards and I am sure we can do the same without any harm.

Our first stop is to look at the history of Bitcoin. The history of Bitcoin is pretty fascinating because there are pre-Bitcoin and post-Bitcoin history. The pre-Bitcoin history touches on the series of events that occurred before Bitcoin was described and presented to the world. You could call this the warm-up if this was a football match.

Secondly, I am going to touch a bit about post-Bitcoin history. I am referring to the series of events that happened after the invention of Bitcoin. Bitcoin was not just invented and everything stopped there. Things changed. Another gold rush emerged. You have probably heard of the "Scramble for Africa" a few centuries ago. Something similar happened when people knew about Bitcoin. Bitcoin changed many things. If redefined what we thought we knew about our monetary system. Importantly, it has laid down the foundation for something far more reaching.

Pre-history of Bitcoin

In my own opinion, the pre-history of Bitcoin starts with the creation of the fiat monetary system and the moment computers were introduced to the world. Each revolution or new era is mainly pioneered by the flaws in the previous system. There may be no flaws sometimes but there is a need to upgrade to a new and better system.

Before the current monetary system of coins and paper notes was introduced, people exchanged goods and services through barter trading. This was a system flawed with so many inconsistencies and unfairness. There was no standard unit upon which goods/services could be measured. It simply thrived on surplus and demand.

It was many years before there was an ingenious idea to invent coins and paper money. A new standard was defined. The current fiat money system was born and it proved to be more efficient than barter trade. Mind you, barter trade still exists today. A few centuries and a couple of decades later, computers were introduced to the world. At the same time, the principle of countries and borders had already been established an in full force. Each country had its own currency whose strength depended on a number of factors. People from different countries could exchange goods and services. Banks were already in place and they could handle such transactions.

On the other hand, the people who were pioneering digital technology were now pushing for digital cash. They wanted to build a digital currency that matched the digital times they were living in. A lot of varied platforms and digital cash protocols were built by many digital experts of the time. David Chaum notably pioneered the ecash protocol, Nick Szabo worked on bit gold while Wei Dai introduced something known as b-money. All these were efforts to find a true digital currency that would replace the fiat monetary system or at least, exist alongside it. These projects were not failures because they laid down the groundwork for what was to come. This is probably a very important period because it is the one that inspired the idea of a digital currency system. However, the technology necessary to build such a cash system was still lacking.

Then in 2008, when hope was faded but not yet completely gone, the internet welcomed a new domain, "bitcoin.org." This was just a simple domain that was to change many things. A few weeks later, the white paper entitled *Bitcoin: A Peer-to-Peer Electronic Cash System* was presented to cryptography experts and enthusiasts. A new currency was being invented in the shadows. This famous white paper was written by an unknown person/programmer by the name Satoshi Nakamoto. The true identity of Satoshi Nakamoto is a big debate that requires a book of its own.

When the Bitcoin network was implemented in 2009, its first users were Hal Finney, Nick Szabo, and Wei Dai. This comes as no surprise as they were the same people who pioneered the groundwork for digital cash long before Bitcoin was conceived. The original creator of Bitcoin, Satoshi, mined close to a million coins of his currency before vanishing into thin air. Gavin Andresen ran the show when the Satoshi bailed out. We don't know if this was a bailout or a strategic exit meant to shield him/her from the public face.

The value of Bitcoin was close to nothing then. People negotiated what they thought was the true value of the coin. There is even a story that a programmer paid for 2 pizzas with 10,000 BTC. Bitcoin had not yet gone mainstream then and I guess the programmer thought he had hit a jackpot. However, slowly, Bitcoin began to grab the attention of many people. To start off, Bitcoin mainly appealed to programmers due to the complex nature of the technology behind it. It is not something that your average Tom, Dick, and Harry would easily understand on any given sunny or rainy day.

2011 was a busy year for Bitcoin. The first fork took place and a new currency was formed. The new currency was called Litecoin. It was spearheaded by Charlie, an ex-employee of Google. Litecoin and a host of other coins that were created that year were known as Altcoins. There were called that because they were simply alternatives to the Bitcoin. Online organizations like WikiLeaks accepted Bitcoins. Bitcoin was now functioning as a currency.

From 2012, many organizations, governments, and government departments took notice of Bitcoin. Bitcoin exchanges were banned in Thailand in 2013. There was a surge in the people who were making transactions using Bitcoin. Bitcoin was becoming more popular and resulted in the creation of several other competing currencies or coins. China's central bank banned the use of Bitcoins. Bitcoin and other cryptocurrencies have had a torrid time in Asian countries with China and Korea being the main culprits. Bitcoin machines were being installed in their thousands in the United States signaling the unofficial acceptance of the digital currency as a medium of exchange.

On the exchanges, the price of Bitcoin was volatile and unpredictable. It would go up and down just like that. One notable thing about Bitcoin is its ability to pick up its price after any major or minor slide. Many people called it a bubble and predicted that it would burst, but each time, it has managed to disappoint them.

Blockchain technology: the main driver behind the success of Bitcoin and cryptocurrencies

Bitcoin is a project that was in the making for many years. Although there isn't much information on the creator of Bitcoin, I can tell you that Bitcoin's success lies partly in blockchain technology. The early attempts to create a digital cash were unsuccessful due to lack of technology that supported the idea. The blockchain is the technology that they were looking for. The word blockchain has been thrown around many times. You hear people talk about it at parties, or over a braai and tech ladies probably talk about at bridal showers. You do not need to feel out of place simply because no one has given you a simple-to-understand yet convincing explanation of the blockchain is.

A blockchain is a distributed public ledger that is used to store and record valuable data and information. The blockchain is governed by the following set of rules:

- Immutable – information entered on the blockchain database cannot be erased or altered.
- Decentralized – this is one of the most attractive attributes of blockchain technology. It is decentralized in the sense that there is no single location where transactions are stored on the network. The transactions exist on every computer on the network. Imagine a situation where we wake to the news that Google servers have been burnt down. The new would be catastrophic but it does not mean the end of the world. You can still search for information on other search engines such as Yahoo and Bing. The internet is not centralized and has no single point of failure. This is how a blockchain network is designed. The only way to take down a blockchain network is to corrupt or destroy all the computers on the network. Trust me, this is not an easy task.
- Transparency – the blockchain network is very transparent due to the fact that every transaction is verified by every computer on the network. The transaction can only be processed if it has been verified by all the members of the network.
- Cryptographically secure – the blockchain network uses the advanced method of cryptography to secure its transactions. This makes the network more secure and less susceptible to attacks and hacks.
- Anonymity – the transactions on the blockchain network are anonymous. Although network users are required to verify each transaction, they have no way of knowing who is making the transaction.

Uses and theories of Bitcoin

Bitcoin is a currency that can be used the same way as the US$ or the Euro. However, it is a currency with a difference. I have talked about its history and revolutionary groundbreaking technology. What I haven't really done is tell you what Bitcoin is and how it works.

Bitcoin is a cryptocurrency that belongs to alternative, digital, and virtual currencies. It is a currency that is generated by computer software and in essence, it may just be a string of zeros and ones. This is because this is how everything in the digital world is presented as. It is alternative in the sense that it an alternative to the current fiat monetary system. Finally, we come to the part that I like most. There is nothing really special about this part. I just enjoy explaining it to people.

It is a virtual currency because this it does not exist in the physical world that same way your paper money and coins exist. No one has ever seen or touched a Bitcoin. Never mind the images you on the internet with a big B. That's not a Bitcoin. Technically speaking, no one owns a Bitcoin. What you simply own is an address to the location of your virtual money. That address has a record of how much currency you have. What you own is a set of private and public keys. The private key is similar to the key to your home or apartment. It's what give you access to your digital currency. It is only known to you. Whoever gets access to your private key has access to your Bitcoins. In the real world, banks and people have safes to keep their money far from prying eyes. You cannot build a safe for your Bitcoins. You can only build a safe for your private keys. Think of your Bitcoins as the money in your bank and the credit card pin number as your private key. Whoever has access to your credit card and pin number also has access to the money in your bank.

The public key is like your bank account. Although you need to keep it safe, it does not matter if it gets in the public eye. In fact, you want it to be in the public eye. The public key is the address to your money. People can only send you Bitcoins through the public key. This is the same way that people send you money using your bank account number.

You can use Bitcoins to make purchases or settle debts. However, the principles are quite different from what you are used to. Let's assume you want to send your child some money or pay for your morning muffins at a local café. This is all that happens.

- A request is lodged with you.
- The request is openly broadcast on the transparent Peer-to-Peer network of computers. Each computer on the P2P network is known as a node.
- The transactions are validated by the network nodes
- The verified and validated transaction is grouped together with other similar transactions. This creates a new data block.
- The newly created block becomes part of the network and this completes the transaction.

Bitcoin transactions

Bitcoin was in a way introduced so that it could address some of the challenges that the banking infrastructure was failing to deliver to the population in the modern times. It is a known fact that sometimes transactions can take as long as 3 -5 business days to clear. This is a long wait especially if you want to use the money for something urgent. Secondly, the transactions are very costly and result in people losing a large chunk of their money. This is one way that banks are profiteering from. Bitcoin aims to correct this in several ways.

- No third-party involved – when you want to send some money to someone, you rely on a bank or other intermediary party to do so. The third-party requires a fee to do this. With Bitcoin, you can send your money to your desired person without worrying about a third party.
- Transaction costs – I just mentioned the cost you pay to an intermediary party who facilitates the transactions. The Bitcoin eliminates the need for a third party with significantly minimizes the money you pay. More importantly, you should be glad to hear to hear that Bitcoin charges near-zero for all the transactions on its network.
- Security – the Bitcoin network is secure due to decentralization. There is no central point that hackers can target before taking down the network. --
- Anonymous – the transactions are anonymous and no one will ever know when you make a transaction. The nodes on the Bitcoin network can only verify the transaction.
- Transaction speed – while banks may take up to 3 days to process a transaction, the same transaction is completed within 10 minutes on the Bitcoin network.

Chapter 2: Ripple

Ripple is one of the popular Altcoins. It is one of the top five cryptocurrencies by market capitalization. Apart from being one of the digital assets that have caused a stir in the financial and investment world, what else can be said about Ripple? There is a lot to talk and write about. My first port of call would be its interesting history. Yes, the history is interesting in the sense that the foundations of Ripple go long back before Bitcoin came into the picture. If you want, you can call it a currency or network that survived in two separate timelines.

The early roots of Ripple are found in Vancouver, Canada. A developer by the name of Ryan Fugger quietly worked on developing the decentralized monetary system. This system, known as Ripplepay, made it possible for people to construct their own currencies. It was not too different from cryptocurrencies that were yet to come. Jed McCaleb was inspired by this system and eventually created the eDonkey network. He was helped by Arthur Britto and David Schwartz to build the network. Probably inspired by Bitcoin and some of its underpinning technologies, the trio started working on building a digital currency protocol similar to Bitcoin. However, it deviated a bit from Bitcoin in that there was no mining involved. This resulted in a huge cut in electricity usage. Secondly, the new system had faster transaction speed compared to Bitcoin. All this work was done in 2011.

The team brought in Chris Larsen in August 2012. Larsen was no stranger in creating online businesses as he had formerly founded E-Loan and Prosper. McCaleb and Larsen held talks with Fugger which resulted in the pair assuming control of Ripplepay. In September of the same year, OpenCoin Inc. was founded. OpenCoin went on to design a new payment system know the Ripple Transaction Protocol. The system borrowed several of its ideas from Fugger's Ripplepay project. The new protocol was very revolutionary and allowed any two parties to send each other money without the need of an intermediary. This marginally reduced the transaction fees and processing time. To add icing on the cake, OpenCoin was backed by several prominent investors such as Google Ventures and Andreessen Horowitz.

McCaleb eventually left Ripple and founded Stellar, a director competitor of Ripple. It is alleged that he left amid disagreements with Larsen. These are only allegations. McCaleb went on to announce that he would be selling all the XRP tokens he owned. That resulted in lawsuits that stopped McCaleb from selling all his tokens at once. It is believed that such an act would have hurt Ripple.

Ripple at a glance

If you have heard of Bitcoin or know what it is, then you have an idea of what Ripple is. Ripple is something similar to Bitcoin but with a different underlying functionality. Ripple may also be confusing because of its dual role. Ripple can refer to a payment protocol or Ripple network's native currency known as the Ripple token (XRP). If you truly want to know what Ripple is, you have to start by make a clear distinction between the two.

The Ripple protocol is an open source global payment network that facilitates global payments at near zero cost and near-instantaneous speed. Ripple is simply in the remittance business. Think of Ripple as the modern Western Union updated with several upgrades. Ripple Company argues that the global payment infrastructure was designed when discos were still the best thing that ever happened to the world. Some of you may not even know what a disco is. There are major flaws in the current payment structure and this is what Ripple intends to address.

To begin with, global transactions take between 3 – 5 days to go through. This is a lot of time by any standards. You have probably heard that "times is money." If this is true, then you can't afford to wait for almost a week before a transaction goes through. Secondly, the cost for such transactions is enormously high. It is estimated by Ripple that people are losing more than $1.6 trillion in annual transaction fees. This is a lot of money that people could keep in their pockets if there is a new system that addresses this issue with the merit it deserves.

You know that "change is the only constant thing in the world." It is high time that there is a change in the payment system. Ripple is that change that people want. Lastly, the current payment system is unreliable and unacceptable.

The Ripple Protocol

The protocol may certainly be a game changer in the global payments sector. The Ripple payment protocol allows you to send and receive any asset of value. This can be gold, fiat money, etc. The Ripple protocol was designed to be adopted by banks to aid them in their global transactions. It has so far been adopted by several banks and financial firms such as American Express.

The actual process that enables Ripple to send money globally is a bit complex. However, I will try to simplify it as much as possible without oversimplifying it. You can understand how Ripple works if we start off with practical examples. Let's say you are in Japan and want to send your friend in Nigeria some money. What normally happens is that the Japanese Yen you deposit into a bank are converted into one of the mainstream currencies such the US$. This conversion incurs conversion expenses. The dollars are sent to the bank in Nigeria. However, the bank in Nigeria can only issue the money in Naira (native currency used in Nigeria) to your friend and not in dollars. The conversion process from US$ to Naira costs some money. You also have to pay the cost of the transaction fee. Moreover, this process takes days to process. In summary, this is a multi-step process that takes time and costs a substantial amount of money.

If you are going to do the same transaction on the Ripple network, you will be doing yourself a big favor. The Ripple protocol looks for the easiest and quickest route to use for such a transaction. The overall goal is to have a near-instantaneous transaction that costs you almost nothing. Ripple simply bypasses some of the steps that you would go through if your use intermediaries for your global transaction.

Let's now go on and try to understand what goes on under the hood of Ripple. I am referring to the actual technology behind technology. The Ripple protocol a Peer-to-peer public ledger system controlled by validating nodes. Transactions on the network are processed by these nodes. A transaction is sent to the Ripple network before it is processed. It is at this point that the Ripple sequence starts. The process is as follows:

- The creation of a new transaction
- The transaction is publicized on the network by all the individual servers. The Ripple server software runs on a server.
- Transactions from all the servers are pooled together so that voting can occur.
- Each transaction must receive a set number of votes before it can proceed to the next round of the process. Transactions that do not receive the minimum number of votes discarded or sent back in line for voting.
- Each transaction needs a minimum of 80% votes. A transaction that achieves this minimum or more becomes part of the ledger.
- The process ends when the transaction gets added to the ledger system.

Difference between Bitcoin and other Altcoins

It is common knowledge that Ripple is a new digital asset that is classified in the same that Bitcoin is classified. Ripple is not very similar to Bitcoin. In fact, there a quite a number of differences between the two. Some of these differences are important in shaping the success of Ripple as a payment protocol and digital currency. Some of the notable differences are outlined below.

- Transaction speed – compared to Bitcoin and other Altcoins, Ripple processes transactions at the speed of light. Transactions that take up to 4 days via conventional banks can take up to 10 minutes on the Bitcoin network to be validated. The same transaction takes only 5 – 10 seconds on the Ripple network. This is insanely fast.
- Method of currency issue – you know that the money in your country is issued and controlled by your central bank. If Bitcoin and Ripple XRP token are a currency, then there should be a way by which they are issued. Bitcoin is obtained by a process known as mining. Mining is an activity that involves solving complex mathematical equations. The miners are rewarded with Bitcoins. The computers used to carry the mining process are very powerful and require a lot of electrical energy.

  Ripple is pre-mined. This basically means that Ripple tokens do not need to be mined the same way that Bitcoins are mined. This saves electrical energy a lot.
- Cheaper costs – the Ripple protocol charges a small fee for carrying out transactions on the network. This fee does not go into anyone's pocket but is rather destroyed. The purpose of the network is to prevent a single entity from 'clogging' the network if the transactions were free. The fee is used as an anti-spam measure.
- The cap on the currency – Bitcoin was designed in such a way that there will ever be 21 million coins in existence. This makes the currency scarce at some point and mining activities will cease to exist. However, Ripple uses a different approach. The

Ripple tokens are destroyed after every transaction and this has a few consequences. The supply of Ripple tokens will start to deflate at some point. The currency will become scarce. There is a major difference between Bitcoin's constant supply of 21 million coins and Ripple's deflating currency.
- Relationship with banks – while Bitcoin and the majority of Altcoins were built to directly compete with banks, the Ripple protocol was built to work with banks. This is where Ripple totally deviates from other digital currencies.
- Decentralization – cryptocurrencies are based on blockchain technology. Blockchain technology allows the digital assets to be decentralized. Decentralization does not support having a central point of authority. The Ripple protocol is not fully decentralized but is making plans to be fully decentralized in the future.

There are major differences between Bitcoin and Ripple. However, they are all grouped as digital assets. Surprisingly though, Ripple is older than Bitcoin, the firstborn of all cryptocurrencies. Just imagine being older than your elder brother/sister. That makes you Ripple.

Chapter 3: Real world examples

Cryptocurrencies have in a way, brought some kind of confusion into the world. But this is the good kind of confusion. It is easy for you to earn a slap on your cheek if you tell someone that Bitcoin is a currency. How can Bitcoin be money? What qualifies it to be treated with the same respect as the US$ or the British Pound. It may be easier to explain this to a younger generation but explaining that to your old grandmother is nothing more than a suicide mission.

However, before I validate that Bitcoin is currency or why it should be treated as such, let's take a trip down a memory lane. A long trip down the memory lane. I will take you on a journey about the history of money. I will look at where we started and how we arrived where we are today. You must always remember that the world has always been controlled by change and evolution.

Money has shown us that it obeys that fundamental trend of the world. The evolution of money is not one that is characterized by greed or ulterior motives, but nature's forces of change. The history of money dates as back as the birth of the world. A long time ago, when the world was still primitive, people had to find a way to trade. Mathematics had not yet been developed and the number system as we know it was not yet developed. Even in those archaic and undesirable conditions, people still needed to find a way to trade.

They found such a way through barter trade. Barter trade is a system in which trade is facilitated by literary exchanging goods. The method obviously had its flaws especially given that there were no standards to govern how exchanges were made. To some extent, the system also relied on supply and demand. If I had excess grain but little fabric, I will go and exchange my grain for fabric. I think problems arose on deciding how much grain was worth a certain amount of fabric.

With time, men became a bit more adventurous and discovered minerals and precious metals. Gold was found to be the most precious of them all. High value was placed on it. It immediately became the new standard method of trade. It surpassed barter trade. Gold became the first currency in the world.

For so many years, gold remained the standard and measure of one's wealth. In the 13th century, the Chinese people invented coins. This was the humble beginning of what we call money today. This new invention had several advantages that led to its gradual and mass adoption. That was the beginning of a new era in the financial world.

Banks came into existence and people had the opportunity to save their money. They even earned an interest on their investments. This was an exciting moment. Money could be sent from one bank to another. Innovation had arrived. People from different countries could conduct businesses with each other with the trust that banks would handle the payment part. And banks did a god job.

But monochromatic televisions were still great. There was no Facebook then. The idea of a smartphone was just a genius' dream. The infrastructure for intercontinental financial transactions was put in place then. Technology and innovation were taking great strides in the right direction. Even in the light of this innovation and accelerated growth, there were still a lot of shortcomings.

The transactions were getting processed at a snail's pace. Transactions took days to be transferred from one country to the next. The prices were for the bank transactions were very high. But nobody complained. It was the choice that people had at the time.

Some of the most visionary people at the time were already working on a new project to invent digital cash. The digital cash would serve the same purpose as fiat money but with some modifications. It was obviously supposed to address the issues of safety, transaction speed, and many more. Many people worked on new ways to create a digital cash. It would be unfair to call these endeavors as complete failures. These are the projects that laid down the foundation for cryptocurrencies.

In 2009, the financial foundations were shaken. Bitcoin was invented. It was introduced to the world. Change and innovation had arrived. Bitcoin lead to the creation of many other Altcoins including Ripple.
The earlier chapters have touched a bit about Bitcoin and Ripple. I will not go over them. However, I will shed more light on a few more issues.

The safety of Bitcoin and Ripple

The safety of Bitcoin and Ripple. It stems from two fundamental questions. Each of the questions carries a lot of weight and needs to be addressed before anyone decides to own any of the cryptocurrencies. The first question is the longtime safety of owning cryptocurrencies. Will Bitcoin and Ripple still be viable in the next coming few years or they will be worth nothing? Secondly, how secure is it to store cryptocurrencies given that the transactions have to be approved by millions of computers on the network? I will address these very important questions methodically.

How can you be guaranteed about the future value of Bitcoin? The short and straight answer is that you cannot. But how did someone who invested in Bitcoin in 2009 or 2010 knew that Bitcoin would be worth almost $20,000 in December 2017? The person didn't know that or even dream of it. But they still went on to invest in it. This is the situation you find yourself in. Should you buy Bitcoins or Ripple? Let's go all over it slowly without including the overwhelming figures.

Bitcoin and Ripple are new currency powered by technology and value. As long as they both continue to serve a purpose and are supported by efficient and relevant technologies, they may live long enough to see the next millennia. I can tell you that Bitcoin and Ripple have changed the way that financial transactions are carried out. And this is only just the beginning. The first half of Bitcoin's nine-year existence has generally been about acceptance and being known to all the people in the world. It was quite difficult at first but it finally has the attention of the world.

It may not be a mainstream currency at the moment but it has made itself known. It has also opened the doors for other cryptocurrencies that are backed by real technology such Ripple. Secondly, Bitcoin has gathered the attention of authorities, regulators, and lawmakers. It has graduated from being the pass time project of computer geniuses to be a topic worth discussing at some of the world's most prestigious events. Think of events like the World Economic Forum. In a way, it is a sign that Bitcoin and Altcoins may become mainstream in the next coming years.

The majority may have heard of the crackdown on Bitcoin exchanges in Asian countries. China was at the forefront of this operation followed by South Korea. Does this spell the doom of Bitcoin and Altcoins? Contrary to the popular belief, this is just the beginning. It shows that Bitcoin is strong enough to gain the attention of authorities. At some point, there has to be regulation on how cryptocurrencies operate in this world. Just keep in mind that they are challenging the territories that have previously belonged to powerful organizations and institutions that have controlled the world for a very long time.

Do I think that Bitcoin will be dumped in the next few years? No. I think that its mass adoption is simply on course. It may not be the mainstream currency in the next few years but its grip on the financial system will increase. It is an investment worth a lot in the future.

The second and equally important question is the safety of owning Bitcoin. Where do you keep them and how do ensure their security? Do you need a safe deposit box for them? Yes, you may need a safe deposit box if you decide to store your Bitcoins in a hardware wallet. How strong is the Bitcoin or Ripple network and how easily can it be attacked? This is where blockchain technology gets interesting?

The safety of Bitcoin depends on the blockchain network. The Bitcoin network is an enormous network of computers running Bitcoin software. Each transaction is controlled and monitored by these computers which are owned by people known as miners. Miners can be added and removed from the network without affecting the network. Each transaction that you carry out on the Bitcoin network is first checked by all the computers on the network. The transaction is validated so as to ensure that there is transparency. Does this make the network impenetrable? No, not at all. The network can be breached and hostage.

This is only true theoretically. In practice, it is a big challenge that will give hackers a good run for its money and computing power. A hacker would have to redo all the work that all the miners on the Bitcoin network do. This requires a lot of power that may not even be compensated by the successful hack. In this regard, it is almost impossible and unthinkable for someone to try and hack the Bitcoin network.

However, there is "A 51% Attack" theory. Mining is now being done by mining pools. A mining pool is a group of miners that work together as a single unit by uniting all their computing power. If a mining pool or single entity can manage to control 51% network, then it can potentially disrupt the entire network. The entity suspends ongoing and legitimate transactions resulting in double spend. Think of double spend as counterfeit money.

The truth is that Bitcoin is a very strong but like any other system, it can be exploited. However, it will be a long time before that happens. In the past, there have been several heists of Bitcoins worth millions. It is important to note that the heists were not as a result of Bitcoin network's weakness but as a result of vulnerabilities found in the wallets storing Bitcoins.

One more thing that you may be wondering about is the anonymity of Bitcoin. Bitcoin is not entirely anonymous. It has been believed to be anonymous because of a number of reasons. These are some of the reasons why Bitcoin has been thought to be anonymous.

Bitcoin addresses are important in carrying out transactions on the network. Unlike bank accounts that are tied to a person's identity, Bitcoin addresses do not require you to produce your personal details.

Bitcoin transactions are not depended on the identity of the people who use the network. They are tied to private and public keys. You can send Bitcoins to someone without them needing to know who you are.

However, it is theoretically possible for the identity of Bitcoin users to be discovered. A person/hacker/official can connect several computers to the Bitcoin network and collate the data to pinpoint where transactions came from. This requires a lot of work but it can be done.

Mining

While the central bank in your country issues and controls the distribution of money, Bitcoins are issued and distributed differently. There is no one entity responsible for the currency issue but rather uses a process known as mining. Mining is done by miners and these people are at the core of the Bitcoin network.

Miners serve two purposes. They solve complex mathematical puzzles with the hope of winning a Bitcoin as the grand prize. Secondly, they validate transactions on the Bitcoin network. Mining is not a simple process but a very complex and energy-intensive process. Miners use energy-hungry to do their job and this comes with a hefty electrical bill.

Some analysts argue that mining is a digital process that turns electrical energy into money.

You may wonder and argue if mining in necessary in the Bitcoin ecosystem. Mining is absolutely necessary because it is the only way of ensuring that new coins are created and distributed on the network. The mining can be done by anyone who has the computing power to do so. This means that there is no central system controlling Bitcoins.

As more and more people chose the mining path, the complexity of the puzzles to be solved has increased. This is to control the number of Bitcoins in circulation. If more people can mine it, the supply might surpass the demand and the value of Bitcoin will decrease. Bitcoin mining is very important. It provides some degree of control in the ecosystem.

The biggest drawback is the high energy consumption which may be contributing to climate change. As of December 2017, it was estimated Bitcoin mining activities require about 31 Terawatt Hours annually. As a result, Bitcoin mining activities use more energy than that used by 159 small individual countries. It is estimated that Bitcoin mining uses more electrical energy than the U.S. in 2019. It is further estimated that Bitcoin mining will match the world's entire energy requirements in 2020. This is where many people believe that Bitcoin is inefficient.

On the other hand, Ripple is not mined but pre-mined. This means that all the Ripple tokens were created before the network was launched. The Ripple creators only release a certain amount of tokens to the public at regular intervals. There are no energy requirements here. Unfortunately, this method defeats the purpose of a decentralized currency.

This means that Ripple tokens are controlled by a few people. These people can crash the market if they want to through pump and dump. The purpose of cryptocurrencies was to decentralize their control so that on one particular person or group of people could have a firm grip on the control of a currency.

However, from an energy point of view, Ripple has better functionality.

Chapter 4: How to buy Bitcoin and Ripple

Buying Bitcoin, Ripple or any other cryptocurrency is not a walk in the park. It is very different from going to the grocery store and buying your favorite items. However, with some knowledge, you can find that buying cryptocurrencies is not that much of a mountain to climb. I will start by saying that you need a digital wallet before buying cryptocurrencies. I will come to that in the next topic chapter.

The best way to buy cryptocurrencies is to use exchanges. I will give you a complete list of exchanges that you can use. There are a few things that you need to be on the look-out for before you choose your preferred exchange.

- Cost and fees – most exchanges will charge for using their services. You need to be aware of these fees before making your first transaction. You don't want to cry foul afterward
- Payment set-up – be sure to check how people are allowed to buy cryptocurrencies. The methods used can be PayPal, bank transfer or debit & credit card. Look for an exchange that accommodated your preferred and convenient method of payment.
- Verification process – some of the major Bitcoin exchanges requires you to verify your identity. Identity verification is important because it protects you from criminal activities. It also allows you to operate in a safe environment.
- Reputation and reviews – take your time to read the reviews of an exchange before signing up. A good website will have positive reviews.
- Compare exchange rates – the exchanges do not operate at the same rate. Look for one with favorable rates.
- Geographic restrictions – the majority of the exchanges limit their services to certain regions and countries. Check to see if your favorite exchange provides its services to people in your region or area.

An exchange is a platform for converting cryptocurrencies or fiat money. Exchanges work differently but the following is common to all of them:

- Have a legal account – open an account with the exchange of your choice. You may be required to verify your identity.
- Deposit fiat or crypto – you will need to buy cryptocurrencies using fiat money or cryptocurrencies. If you want to buy cryptocurrencies for the first time, it is better to settle for exchanges that accept fiat money.
- Withdrawal – you can send your cryptocurrencies to a new and safe crypto address.

There are, as expected, some differences between the hundreds of exchanges out there. You must take note of the differences as they are very important. Your job is to seek an exchange that is aligned with your short-term and long-term goals.

- Coins supported – exchanges don't support the same coins. Others only specialize in Bitcoins while others the major coins such as Ethereum, Ripple, and Litecoin. Be sure of the coins that you want to buy first and check if the exchanges have support for your coins.
- Fiat support – go for exchanges that support payment through credit/debit cards or bank transfers.
- Fees charged – this is particularly important. You do not want to lose your money over some high charges. Exchanges can either charge you for trading through their platform or making withdrawals and deposits.
- Exchange types – there are three types of exchanges.
    - Broker – brokers buy cryptocurrencies from exchanges and sell them on their own and usually higher price. They will obviously be expensive to buy from but the process is simple.
    - Trading platforms – this is a trading platform with advanced algorithms to trade cryptocurrency pairs.

- P2P marketplace – a P2P marketplace is interesting in the way it functions. It matches buyers and sellers together. It does not process any transaction.

I have compiled a short list of some of the popular exchanges that you can use to buy and sell your cryptocurrencies.

Coinbase

Coinbase was established in 2011 by Fred Ehrsam and Brian Armstrong. The exchange began offering its services in 2012. It is estimated that the California-based exchange has more than 13.3 million users of November 2017. It accepts fiat currencies from 32 countries and provides its services to residents of more than 190 countries globally. The exchange deals with Bitcoin, Ether, Bitcoin Cash, and Litecoin.

Coinbase allows you to buy cryptocurrencies with a debit or credit card and bank transfers. Coinbase requires you to do a full identification verification. This includes uploading your ID document as well as latest proof of residence.

The exchange has limits on the amount you transact per day. A verified U.S. person can transact Bitcoins worth $50,000 per day. European customers are required to have a maximum balance of €30,000 in their Coinbase account. Coinbase allows you to create a wallet that you can use to keep your wallet. As a side rule, store your digital wealth far away from exchanges.

Coinmama

Coinmama is an Israeli-based Bitcoin exchange. It is famous for accepting payments through credit and debit cards. However, it charges a high fee of 6%. It serves a large number of countries except for a few that are under sanctions.

It has been in the industry for quite a long time. You can make transactions worth $150 or less (in Bitcoins) without verifying your

ID. You need to an ID verification if you want to make bigger transactions. The exchange enables you to make daily purchases that are not worth more than $5,000 in Bitcoins. Your monthly limit is $20,000.

Poloniex

Poloniex was established in 2014 by Tristan D'Agosta. The exchange was hacked in the same year and lost 12.3% of customer Bitcoins. Ever since then, the company has tirelessly to improve its security. It currently stores all cryptocurrencies in cold storage. It only keeps enough cryptocurrencies to facilitate daily trading. The exchange has an auditing program that constantly monitors the platform. The aim is to pick any strange activities before they cause a major problem. The platform's 2-Factor Authentication is a good security feature.

The exchange allows you to buy, send, and trade over 100 currencies including Bitcoin and Ripple. Coinmama charges depending on the Bitcoin amount being transacted. Transactions can take as long as 30 minutes to 1 hour to be completed.

The withdrawal limit on the platform is based on verification. Unverified account holders can only withdraw up to $2,000. Verification increases the limit amount to $25,000. The verification process requires your ID, proof of address and sometimes, your selfie holding your ID credentials.

There is a higher level of verification that can allow withdrawing more than $25,000. The best place to find this information is to contact the platform's support center.

Kraken

Kraken was founded in 2011 in San-Francisco. The exchange allows trading in Euro, US dollar, Canadian dollar, Japanese yen, and the British pound. Kraken has managed to expand over the years due to its ability to its acquisition of companies such as CryptoWatch.

Kraken is a notable exchange because it is trusted by the Japanese government and has the blessing of European banks.

The platform is conducive for professional traders due to its liquidity, rich features, and its speed. It is very secure and transparent. It allows you to buy a variety of currencies including Bitcoin, Ripple, Ether, Litecoin, Bitcoin Cash, Ether Classic, EOS, etc.

The exchange does not allow payments through PayPal and debit and credit cards. However, wire transfers are allowed. Wire transfers are processed within 1 – 5 business days. Kraken is known for its low transaction fees.

Kraken requires you to verify your identity before you can start buying cryptocurrencies. You will have to provide your ID document and proof of residence.

Blockchain.info

Blockchain.info wallet is an online wallet that you can use using any browser of your choice. It also has a mobile version that you can use. The online version has a 2-Factor-Authentication (2FA) which makes it more secure.

The blockchain is a popular wallet and can be used to store Bitcoin and Ethereum. It has an easy-to-use wallet. It has an informative bar at the bottom that allows users to see the number of daily transactions. Some of its major selling points include:

- Blockchain.info is one of the most well-known companies in the crypto industry
- Suited for small regular payments
- Easy to use
- The smartphone makes the wallet more interesting to use

Chapter 5: How to store

In the real world, you store your fiat money in bank accounts, safes, pockets, or wallets. Cryptocurrencies are stored slightly differently. They are stored in digital wallets. I will go over the definition of a digital currency before telling you what a digital wallet.

A cryptocurrency is a virtual currency that you can neither touch nor feel. It is simply a record of transactions. You don't really own the currency. What you simply own is the public and private keys. The public key is the address you give people to send you money while the private key allows you access to your money.

A digital wallet is simply a software program or hardware that allows you to generate public and private keys. It receives your digital cash and allows you to spend it. There are two types of storage. Hot and cold. Hot storage refers to any wallet that stores your private keys online. This is a bit dangerous as it exposes your wealth to hackers and attackers. Cold storage means the opposite. It is any digital wallet that is not connected to the internet.

There are several types of wallets. Let's go over them.

Desktop wallet

This is a wallet program installed on your desktop or laptop. You can only access on the machine that it was installed on. You can only lose your money if you lose your gadget. Fortunately, the majority of desktop wallets now come with backup plans. A desktop wallet is a secure option.

Exodus is a good example of a desktop wallet. Although considered to be an online wallet, the Exodus wallet supports several coins including Bitcoin, Ethereum, EOS, etc. The wallet also supports several fiat currencies including the US dollar, Japanese Yen, etc.

The wallet allows you to back up your data which is a good security measure. The wallet has a customizable interface. However, the only drawback is that it is an online wallet and should not be used to store a large amount of money.

Another desktop wallet you can use is the Jaxx wallet. It was developed by Anthony Diiorio, Ethereum co-founder. It is compatible with Windows, Mac, and Android. You can use it across multiple devices. It stores Bitcoin, Ethereum, Zcash, and others.

Mobile

This is a mobile wallet that you can download and install on your phone. A mobile wallet is not different from your traditional wallet. You can travel with it and make purchases on the go. Mobile wallets are slightly risky as it is easy to lose your smartphone.

Online wallets

Online wallets are programs that store your wealth online. You can access the wallets using any device connected to the internet. This gives you convenience but poses a great security risk. Online wallets can also include exchanges. It is always a good idea to store only a small portion of your money in online wallets.

A good example of an online wallet is the Bitpanda wallet. You can use the wallet to buy, sell, and store several coins such as Bitcoin, Ripple, Dash, Litecoin, Ethereum, and Bitcoin Cash. The wallet is free to use. It has a simple user interface that will get you going in no time.

Hardware

This is the kind of wallet you should have when you own a lot of cryptocurrencies. Hardware wallets are hardware devices solely dedicated to storing your crypto wealth. It is very secure as your wallet is stored offline.

The Ledger/Trezor wallet is among the top hardware wallets you can buy. It allows you to store Bitcoin, Ripple, Stellar, Litecoin, and several other coins. It has a built-in display screen that allows you to see and confirm transactions. You can also connect it to a computer via a USB connection. It is secure and allows you to recover your money in case you lose your wallet.

Paper

A paper wallet keeps the copy of your private keys on paper. You can then store the paper in a secure place such as a safe. A paper wallet can have a barcode that you scan. This will allow you to send and receive money. A paper wallet is a secure wallet option as it keeps your private keys away from the public domain.

The Cryo Card wallet is a good paper wallet that can secure your money in cold storage. The wallet has the shape and feel of credit/debit card. It is made of stainless steel. It is secure and can withstand fire, floods, acids, bases, temperatures, and salt water. It supports Bitcoin.

Chapter 6: Before investing

Cryptocurrencies would not have attracted so much attention if they did not allow people to invest in them and reap 'real' rewards. I call them real rewards because some investors have made north of 1,000% in investment returns. I am sure you are familiar with such stories. Bitcoin started without any value nor any promise of it.

In time, people caught the Bitcoin fever and nine years later, we are where we are today. 1 Bitcoin is worth more than $10,000. That's a lot. There is even speculation and expectation for it to go even higher. Some analysts have suggested that it may reach as high as $100,000 in the next few years. Nothing is impossible with Bitcoin.

This is the reason why many people invest in it. And we wouldn't be surprised if you want to.

Big disclaimer:
You will get a marathon journey about investing in Bitcoin or Ripple. However, I have to make it clear from the onset that I am not a financial advisor. I am not a Wall Street expert. I have learned over the years that the investment world is not generous and fair at all. The information you find in this book is not professional advice. Do not rely on it to make investments. However, you can use it in conjunction with your own research and due diligence.

Let's immediately dive into the world of crypto investments.

Investment mindset

Investing is not an activity that you can engage in without the right frame of mind. Even the most successful investors such as Warren Buffet, Paul Tudor Jones, George Soros, etc. do not just invest anyhow. They first need to get the right investment mindset. This is the mindset that I am going to be writing about. The mindset of a winning investor.

You first need to understand that you are an investor and not a gambler. So, what's the difference between the two? Approach and attitude.

A gambler thrives and survives on luck. An investor survives on informed decisions. Your first priority as an investor is to get as much as information before you make a decision. There is nothing like a safe investment. Every investment activity involves some risk and the potential to lose some or all of your money. An intelligent and successful investor takes calculated risks.

"Until you can manage your mind, do not expect to manage money."
Warren Buffet

What kind of a mindset do you then need in order to become a successful investor?

Commitment

Needless to say, there are a few things that can be achieved without commitment. The first you need is a commitment to your investment career or part-time activity. This is not something you should partake after a disappointing day at work or when you have had a fight with your loved ones.

You need to approach this seriously. This means that you need to do all the necessary and sometimes dirty work of researching what you want to research in. Tell yourself that you are in for the long term. Always remember your end goal. This will always push you to stay in the game even when there is no reason to.

It becomes more important when it comes to investing in cryptocurrencies. Cryptocurrencies are highly volatile. They need people with a steady mind and are not easily moved by market changes.

Keep your emotions in check

Emotions are the biggest downfall of the majority of traders and investors. Do not attach yourself to a particular coin or token. Only invest in a coin that is worth investing in.

Know when to exit and when to continue in the game. Be strong enough to stick to your game plan. The truth is that things will not always go your way. There are times when you will lose your investments. It has happened to thousands of people and it might happen to you. However, that should not control you or instill fear in you.

If an investment is not going your way, decide if you should exit or hold for some time. Be sure to keep your emotions out of an investment decision you make.

Do not invest in new tokens/coins simply because your previous investment did not go well. This quick desire to "fix things" can only lead to more damage. Instead, take your time to study what went wrong. Give your emotions time to cool down. Emotional decisions are not always the best logical ones. Investing requires logic and not emotions.

Have a solid strategy

It is one thing to have a good idea and it is another to execute that idea brilliantly. There are so many coins/tokens that you invest or trade.

How then do you hedge yourself against losing your investment?

You need to be observant before you start investing or picking out your perceived digital winners. Develop a hypothesis on how to pick your winners. Test it if possible and if time allows.

Cryptocurrencies have played their part in minting new and unexpected millionaires. It can do the same for you. This doesn't come easily though. You need to know how to spot the winning opportunities.

Only go investments or trades that offer you decent returns with minimum risk. The market is already risky. There is no need to add more risk to it.

This is a country road. It will get dusty and nasty. You should be prepared for that beforehand. Take risks where possible.

You will make mistakes

No one wants to hear this but you have to hear it. You are not a machine. You will make mistakes at some point. This is unavoidable. What is avoidable is repeating the same mistake over and over again.

> *"The greatest mistake you will ever make is making the same mistake twice."*

Whenever you make a mistake, acknowledge it. Write it down. Mistakes take you on a path of discovery. Learn and grow from them. You can never know it all if you are an investor. You are on a path of discovery and making money.

Be your own person

The one-size-fits-all rule does not apply to all investors. Each one has his/her own signature investment/trading philosophy. You need to have your own.

Don't ride the train that others ride. Be prepared to walk in the desert if you have to. Do not be afraid of being uncomfortable if you have to.

Only associate yourself with people who share the same vision as you. Avoid being around people who instill negative thoughts in you.

You can only be you if you associate with people who allow you to be your own kind of investor. Learn from your mistakes. Experience is the biggest teacher. Learn from it. Let is shape you as an investor.

Be a unique investor/trader. You don't have to be ashamed of it.

Be passionate

Many people invest for the sole purpose of making money. There is nothing wrong with this. We all need money to survive.

Investing is not a stroll in the park. You may lose money along the way. You will likely lose some of your money too.

You will quit at the first hurdle if you are not prepared for this.

You have to be passionate about investing. This is what will keep you going when things are not going your way. Passion takes beyond the wall that stops the majority from crossing over to the other side.

Passion will stop you from quitting. Passion and discipline are what you need to be successful.

Putting it all together

These are not the ten commandments of the mindset of an investor. They are the guidelines that will help you find your true self in the investment world. Put these traits to use. Keep on searching who you are.

You can only find success when you find your true space in the universe. You are a star. Find your position in the sky and you will be able to give some light to the world.

Your light is your success as an investor.

Paper profits vs. actual profits

Your main aim as an investor is to make profits. You are not that different from someone who is running a business. You are similar in the sense that you put your capital on the line, carry out an activity with the hope of realizing a profit.

Business profits/losses are different from investment profits/losses. I will constantly refer to profit because our collective aim is to make huge profits. Who wants to lose anywhere?

As an investor, you buy your stock or cryptocurrency and hold it in your investment portfolio. The next thing you do is track its price changes. If its prices become higher than the prices you bought it for, you have made a profit. However, you can't access the profit yet or use it. It is a profit that only exists on paper.

This profit is not yet secure. It can change anytime. It can go up or down. It signifies that you are still in the game. And being in the game means that you are exposed to more profits or running a loss. You cannot spend this profit.

In simple terms, its profit you have but don't own yet. However, it is entirely up to you to decide when you want to cash out.

The moment you decide to cash out is the moment you have actual profit. This is the profit you actually have and use as you wish. I like to call it the hard profit because it is tangible, usable, and distributable.

There is a bad side to paper profits. They can make you a theoretical billionaire/millionaire but in reality, you may even struggle to pay your bills. Some rules and clauses in your stock/option contract may prevent you from liquidating your investment until a certain time. You may even lose your paper profit before you realize it. The dot-com boom produced poor "paper millionaires". This is because they held stocks and securities that were profitable. However, the law prevented them to sell the stock in their portfolio until a certain. The dotcom bubble popped and the theoretical millionaires were back at square one.

There are also paper losses. They are not different from paper profits except that you are in the red. The bone of contention is what you should do with paper losses. Some people argue that you should hold them with the hope that they will turn into profits. This is a good idea but risky as well. Your losses may sink deeper.

A successful investor should know how to deal with losses as much he/she knows how to deal with profits. There are times when it makes more sense to cash out your paper losses and turn them into actual losses.

For the record, I hate losses of any kind. There are times when they are unavoidable. This critical situation requires quick thinking and great decision making. Let's take a look at some of the moments when it makes sense to realize your paper losses rather than holding them.

Avoid further losses

Cashing out early on will prevent you from incurring further losses as the price of the stocks or crypto coin. Some coins are scams. Many of them are defunct. It is better to salvage a portion of your investment capital than to walk away empty-handed.

Have more cash

If your coin continues on a downward trend and you are assured that it may not turn things around, cash out and have more money to diversify your portfolio.

Sharpen your thinking

Going through some losses will sharpen your thinking. It will cause you not to blindly invest in any coin or stock without conducting due diligence. If you did your part to the latter and the coin still resulted in you registering a loss, all you have to do is walk away while you can. Sharpen your mind while you wait for the next coin to invest in.

A paper loss is an elephant in the room

A paper loss affects your thinking. The pain you feel reduces your productivity and might affect your ability to make profitable investments in the future. Taking it out of the picture may give cause to see things differently. You won't have anything to weigh you down.

Special note on cryptocurrencies

Cryptocurrencies are highly volatile. This is a basic rule you must know when investing in them. Paper losses should not put you in panic mode when you have invested in cryptocurrencies. Be patient. The prices may adjust themselves and you end up on a winning.

Don't be quick to cash out on paper losses.

Long-term investing vs. day trading

Think of investing and day trading as two different routes that lead you to the same destination. The common goal of investing or trading is to accumulate wealth through buying stocks, crypto coins/tokens, etc. and holding them for a certain period until they appreciate in value. The only difference between the two is how long you hold the coins/tokens in your portfolio until you sell.

The million dollar question is probably which one is better between the two.

The actual answer depends on a number of factors. I will simply list the pros and cons of each and you will decide for yourself which one is better. Sometimes, you have to make your own choices depending on the available information. What works for Jane does not necessarily have to work for John.

Investing

Investing in cryptocurrencies is known as HODLing. The investors are known as HODLers. HODL simply stands for Hold On for Dear Life. Investing allows to have a portfolio of tokens/coins and hold them for a long time. The holding period allows you to earn profits.

Here are the pros of investing or HODLing:

- You are not affected by the daily fluctuations of the market – cryptocurrencies are very volatile. HODLing gives you peace of mind as your aim is to make profits in the long run.
- HODLing can be profitable even for first-time investors. All they have to do is buy, hold, and cash out when the markets are attractive.
- No emotions. Longtime investments automatically keep your emotions in check. You do not need to check the market movements on a daily basis (though some do that). Any decline in the market is not likely going to affect you.
- Effortless. You don't need to put a lot of effort as compared to day trading. It also does not require much time commitment as compared to day trading. However, you still need to do your due diligence before investing to make sure that you are picking coins/tokens that will be profitable in the long run.

Here are the few cons of investing

- You may miss out on daily market jumps

Day trading

Day trading is not for the faint of heart. Here are some pros for crypto day trading.

- Compounding. You can quickly grow your investment capital by pouring in your profits for today in tomorrow's trades.
- You can make an instant profit from daily market movements.

Its cons are as follows:

- Not suitable for beginners as it carries a lot of risks. It can result in the complete loss of your investment capital in a short space of time.
- Requires more time per day. You have to dedicate a portion of daily time to trading.
- Involves a lot of emotions due to market movements that happen each day.
- You may be trading against bots and machines. The odds won't be in your favor.
- The attention and hard work required may add some stress to your life.
- High transaction fees. A chunk of your investment and profit is swallowed in transaction fees due to the several trades and transactions you carry out on a single day.

Investment/trading techniques

There are several techniques you can use in your investment/trading strategy. However, it is important that you understand each technique so that you can use it to your advantage. I have listed a few techniques below.

Fundamental analysis

Fundamental analysis is simply the application of economics, investor sentiment, and current events to determine the price or future price of the crypto markets.

The fundamental analysis of cryptocurrencies is totally different from the fundamental analysis of public companies. This is because of the differences between cryptocurrencies and public companies. Moreover, the crypto market is still young and there is a long way to go in analyzing crypto tokens/tokens. Fortunately, there are some ways that you can use to determine if a token/coin is worth investing in. These include:

- Token/coin value or utility
- News and publicity

I will now go over each of the points above in detail.

Value or utility

A good coin/token must do something unique. It should solve a problem. This is one easy way to see if a coin/token will still be useful in the next five or ten years.

Ask yourself this question, what does the question do? You can get this answer from reading and analyzing their white paper. The white paper should be fairly technical without any sort of marketing or fake promises.

If you can ascertain that a coin can solve a problem, then it may be worth looking at. You also need to consider the people behind the currency. This includes both the technical and executive team.

You then need to consider the coin's roadmap. Check what the coin initially aimed to achieve and what they have achieved so far. This can be easily interpreted by looking at how much they raised in the ICO and how they spent it.

If at some point you feel that the coin/token may be a scam, then it may be one. A real project does not many red flags if it does at all. Fundamental analysis is all about checking if a coin has one or more red flags. Stay away from those coins.

News and publicity

Avoid any coin/tokens that are associated with bad publicity. A good project should be in the news for the right reasons.

A good project must be in the news for its progress. It must be mentioned for its worthiness and how it can contribute significantly to solving problems.

Technical analysis

Technical analysis is an investing/trading technique that forecasts future market prices based on historical data such as prices, trading volume, market cap, etc. Technical analysis is mainly used by day traders.

The technical analysis predicts the future using past data. The most important aspect of this technique is to pick up trends and make decisions based on those trends. Technical analysts use bar charts, candlesticks, and statistics to make their decisions.

Averaging down

There are times when you buy a coin and suddenly it drops its price. This is the case if you have been following the crypto market lately. Some investors employ the "averaging down" technique as a way to minimize the potential loss and maybe even make a profit.

The best way to understand averaging down is to illustrate it by means of simple mathematics. Let's assume that you decide to buy coin XYZ at a price of $5/coin. You pay $500 for 100 coins. The price falls to $2.50 shortly after. In theory, you have made a paper loss of 50%.

This prompts you to buy more shares at the low rate. You buy extra 100 shares at $250. Together, you have bought 200 coins at $750. The new average price of the coin is $3.75. If the coin picks up and makes it to $4, then you have made an "average profit" on all your 200 coins. You can sell them for $800 leaving you with a profit of $50.00.

Is averaging down a good strategy? Yes and no is the answer.

There are several factors that necessitate a price drop. The coin may not increase in the short term. The price may even fall down further. This will leave you with further losses. Averaging down also allows your "bruised ego" to sink you deeper. It may seem like a way out but actually, it's a way to take away more money from you.

On the other hand, averaging down may lead to a price increase. Even if the coin does not make it past $5 (your initial investment), you still make a profit.

All in all, you need to be careful before you think of averaging down. It may be a good strategy since the crypto market is very volatile.

Pump and dump strategies

Tokens are not created equal. Not all creators of cryptocurrencies can be trusted. Some just want to cash on the hype. The cold and harsh truth is that there are scams out there. It is your duty to recognize or smell them from afar and stay as far away as possible.

Some creators develop a coin and keep as many coins as possible for them. This basically gives them the power to control the market and even crash it if they want to. They will hold their substantial stake while they create some hype around the coin.

When the coin fetches a higher price, they can sell all their coins. This floods and crashes the market. Such a strategy is known as a pump and dump scheme.

The good news is that you can avoid it. You have to analyze the coin and find out the portion reserved for the development team. Be careful of projects where the development team control a substantial amount of the coins/tokens. It sort of centralizes the currency and gives them the power to crash if they want to.

Governmental measures and policies on cryptocurrencies

We all knew that it was a matter of time before governments began to notice the attention that cryptocurrencies are getting and do something about it. Governments do something by passing laws and adopting new policies that either promote or prohibit the new tech in question.

Cryptocurrencies seem to have been on the radar of some influential countries in the past few months. This came off the back of Bitcoin trading as high as $19,000+ in December 2017. It could be one of the factors that triggered some governments to act.

China was the main actor. It cracked down on Bitcoin exchanges citing the currencies to be illegal. This also spiraled to other countries such as South Korea. South Korea took a similar stance as China. The Indian government has indicated that there is a need for the cryptocurrency market to be regulated.

The regulation itself may not be a bad idea. Some are in favor of it because they believe that there are scam ICOs that are conning people their money. A government intervention would solve this.

Another section of cryptocurrency users claims that governments are trying to take control of cryptocurrencies the same way they control fiat money. This does not sit well with them.

There are also some countries like Venezuela that have gone to the extent of creating their own digital currencies. Venezuela recently launched the Petro token which is backed by oil and gas. This has sparked some controversy from within the borders of the country. The main political opposition party is accusing the government of creating the digital currency in order to cover up its mess.

Internationally, some countries are not endorsing the move as they believe that it allows Venezuela to circumvent sanctions imposed on it. Some countries are considering having their own cryptocurrencies. These include China and Iran.

The truth is that there is a long way to go before governments can fully enact policies that will either monitor or ban cryptocurrencies altogether. In the meantime, cryptocurrencies have a promising future and may even be legal tender in several countries in the next few years.

Putting it altogether

Be warned that investing in cryptocurrencies carries high risk and be cautious. I encourage you not to invest blindly. You have to do your due diligence before putting your money away. The crypto market is young and volatile. You can make huge profits or easily lose all your life savings.

You can minimize the risk by following an investment protocol. This involves doing thorough research in as many coins as possible. You then narrow it down to a few potential winners. Invest in a diverse number of coins.

Never put all your eggs in one basket.

Lastly, only invest money that you can afford to lose. Do not invest your entire salary or money that you need for paying your bills. That money can be wiped away in an instant. Lastly, be in the right frame of mind before you start investing. Learn to control your emotions. Investing, if not done properly, can ruin you the same way that gambling has ruined several people.

On the bright side, investing or trading cryptocurrencies has produced millionaires. You can be the next millionaire. Avoid being counted among losers.

Chapter 7: Who is the winner, Bitcoin or Ripple?

It is common that many people ask which one is the better token/coin between Bitcoin and Ripple. Let's briefly take a look at each coin and what purpose it serves.

I will start off with Bitcoin, the big brother. Bitcoin is considered to be a "store of value." This, in a certain way, puts on the same par as fiat currency. This is not surprising because it has already been called the "digital gold." It has some similarities to gold. It can be used as a currency. Many people are now aware of it and its potential.

Some big institutions such as central banks and governments are afraid of it. They ought to be. Bitcoin is slowly changing the way we send, receive, and store money. Central banks are known for being the custodians of fiat money and Bitcoin is particularly threatening their own existence.

This obviously will not sit well with them. They will try to monitor it and regulate it in order to stop it from becoming a mainstream currency.

On the other hand, Ripple seems to be doing well in forming partnerships with banks. The Ripple protocol was specifically designed for banks. There is a general argument that it is partially centralized. Ripple and Bitcoin are fundamentally different. Bitcoin is a currency while Ripple is a utility token. It is then difficult to compare the two. More importantly, they are not in direct completion. In fact, Ripple complements Bitcoin. These two are meant to co-exist together in the financial ecosystem.

There is no winner between Ripple and Bitcoin. They both serve their purpose well.

Thank you!

A gift as a thank you!

The cryptocurrency world is a fast moving world. Knowledge is power and the world of the cryptocurrencies keeps evolving.

If you want to stay up-to-date, please check out the author's website:

www.aboutcryptocurrencies.net.

Here you will find the latest cryptocurrencies news gathered from around the world and updated multiple times per day. Sign-up for the 'Daily Crypto News' and receive the electronic version of the officially published book: 'Bitcoin: What is Bitcoin?' for free as a thank you for buying this book.

So go to www.aboutcryptocurrencies.net, sign up and get the **ebook for free** as a thank you.

Finally, if you enjoyed this book, then I'd like to ask you for a favor, would you be kind enough to leave a review for this book on Amazon? It'd be greatly appreciated!

To leave a review for this book on Amazon use the below link:

https://www.amazon.com/dp/1986978737/

Thank you for reading and I want to wish you the best in the world of cryptocurrencies.

And you know, only make educated decisions!

Yours sincerely,

Johan von Amsterdam

Other books in the series

Monero vs Bitcoin
The battle of the cryptocurrencies

Cryptocurrencies; the revolutionary technology that has brought with it dynamism to the financial sector and an evolution to all sectors. Through easing transactions and other data collation mechanisms, their wide reaching architecture is expected to have ramifications on all business spheres long into the future.

- However, do we really understand what cryptocurrencies are?
- Are we knowledgeable on their implications on business?
- Do we know the different cryptocurrencies and their differences?

This book seeks to answer these questions. It begins by introducing readers to the field after which it drills down to the intricacies and finally get to specific currencies: Bitcoin and Monero. It concludes its discussion giving direction to readers on which cryptocurrency would be best under different circumstances.

The book will certainly give readers a deep understanding of Bitcoin and Monero.

Expand your knowledge today and buy this book now:

https://amzn.to/2E5IWAx

or search for: 'Monero vs bitcoin'.

www.ingramcontent.com/pod-product-compliance
Lightning Source LLC
Chambersburg PA
CBHW030052230526
45471CB00003B/1066